M000203152

The Art of

SPACE JAM ™

The Art of

SPACE JAM ™

Edited by
Charles Carney &
Allen Helbig

RUTLEDGE
HILL PRESS

WORLDWIDE PUBLISHING

Published in Nashville, Tennessee, by Rutledge Hill Press, Inc.,
211 Seventh Avenue North, Nashville, Tennessee 37219.

Distributed in Canada by H. B. Fenn & Company, Ltd., 34 Nixon Road,
Bolton, Ontario L7E 1W2.
Distributed in Australia by Millennium Books, 33 Maddox Street, Alexandria NSW 2015.
Distributed in New Zealand by Tandem Press, 2 Rugby Road, Birkenhead, Auckland 10.
Distributed in the United Kingdom by Verulam Publishing, Ltd.,
152a Park Street Lane, Park Street, St. Albans, Hertfordshire AL2 2AU.

Designed by David Kaestle, Inc.,
New York, New York.

Library of Congress Cataloging-in-Publication Data

The art of Space jam / edited by Charles Carney and Allen Helbig.
        p.   cm.
    ISBN 1-55853-427-X (hardcover)
        1. Space jam.   2. Animated films—United States.   3. Warner Bros.
Inc.   I. Carney, Charles.   II. Helbig, Allen.
NC1766.U53S593   1996
791.43'3—dc20   96-30957
                                                         CIP

Printed in Mexico

1 2 3 4 5 6 7 8 9—99 98 97 96

To the international team of *Space Jam* artists, whose great individual talents are subsumed into a brilliant whole, this book is humbly dedicated.

Acknowledgments

This book would not have been possible except for the strenuous efforts of the staff at *Space Jam* Animation, notably Warner Bros. Feature Animation president Max Howard, producer Ron Tippe, co-directors of animation Tony Cervone and Bruce Smith, and the unflappable Mitch Ferm. We also extend our sincerest thanks to Ivan Reitman and Joe Medjuck, David Kaestle, Amy Inouye and Future Studio, Gabe Lakatosh, Gina Misiroglu, Skye Van Raalte-Herzog, and, in no way least, Michael Harkavy.

Contents

Introduction

Part 1: The Scene

Part 2: The Jams

Part 3: The Ultimate Game

Introduction

The *Art of Space Jam* is a gallery of — fancy this — *Space Jam* art, though not necessarily finished, screen-quality material. The editors have purposely selected many of the orphan sketches, the oddball takes, tossed-out concepts, doodling, and thoughtful drawing, all of which contribute to what you see on the screen. The intent behind this book is to show the artists' work as if peeking into their notebooks or glancing over their shoulders as they draw.

The questions artists ask themselves are answered in sketches, just as the questions writers ask themselves are answered in essays. The artists *attempt* to convey something rather than purport to make a definitive statement. What would a place like Moron Mountain look like? What kinds of tacky amusements would reflect the soul of its

Conceptual Bang Nerdluck by Paul Chung

Conceptual Lola Bunny by Jerry Rees

owner, the cigar-grinding Swackhammer? And what of Swackhammer himself? How should he be cast? What would Michael Jordan find when he's dragged into Looney Tune Land? The world of William Burroughs, or of Thornton Wilder? What would a Nerdluck look like? How would he move? What should be his mode of travel? More baffling — what should a Nerdluck look like after he has been transformed into a Monstar? Should the Monstars be frightening or comical? And what about this Lola Bunny? What's the attraction for Bugs? Cerebral? Corporal? Animal, vegetable, or mineral?

The art presented here is the "what if" as much as the "this is it."

There is fire to this work, impulse sparking off the end of a sharpened pencil. Animators are funny people, silent comedians whose humor springs from a keen sense of absurdity, visual timing, and an absolute command of their art. Some of the pieces are brilliantly unpolished, like raw pearls. Some are broad, some subtle. Some, though they act merely as backgrounds for the boisterous Looney Tunes, are curiously thought-provoking when isolated. These works come from a variety of studios worldwide, most of whose artists have never met their counterparts from a sister studio, yet their work is thoroughly collaborative, as one viewing of *Space Jam* will make very clear. It's no easy task creating animation that can keep up with the electrifying Michael Jordan. This they have accomplished, and then some.

Conceptual Bupkus Monstar by Bruce Smith

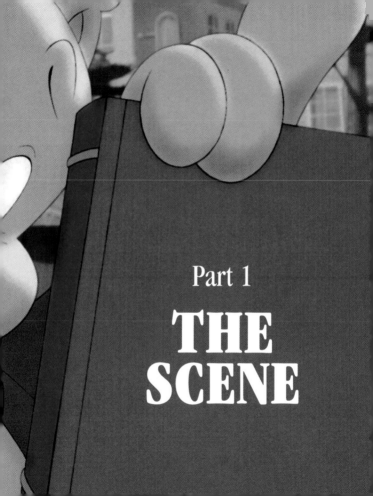

Part 1

THE SCENE

Conceptual Moron Mountain planet by Davy Liu

Overleaf: Conceptual Moron Mountain planet by Bill Wray

Overleaf: Conceptual Moron Mountain planet by Mark Whiting

Moron Mountain is a decaying amusement park in outer space, desperately in need of some amusements. Its ruthless, cigar-chewing CEO, Swackhammer, would love to infuse his lame acreage with some new life.

Conceptual Moron Mountain park entrance by Dan McHugh

Conceptual Moron Mountain park entrance by Bill Wray

Overleaf: Conceptual Moron Mountain park entrance by Dan McHugh

In his dark, forbidding office at Moron Mountain, the old business shark knows he can get his attractions the old fashioned way: steal them. And what better attraction to steal than planet Earth's own beloved Looney Tunes?

vackhammer rough animation by Rob Stevenhagen

Conceptual Swackhammer's office by Neil Ross

Conceptual Swackhammer's office by Neil Ross

Conceptual Swackhammer's office by Don Reich

Swackhammer and minion rough animation by Vladimir Todorov

Conceptual Swackhammer by Uli Meyer

Conceptual Swackhammer by Dan Root

Conceptual Swackhammer by Vincent Woodcock

Swackhammer rough animation by Rob Stevenhagen

Swackhammer rough animation by Rob Stevenhagen

He sends his bullied henchmen, the tiny Nerdlucks, to do his dirty work. After all, it's steady employment for the Looney Tunes. They'll perform at Moron Mountain forever — for free, of course.

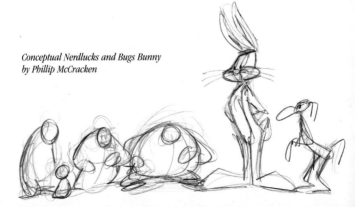

Conceptual Nerdlucks and Bugs Bunny by Phillip McCracken

Conceptual Bupkus Nerdlucks by Paul Chung

Conceptual Nerdlucks by Uli Meyer

Conceptual Nawt Nerdlucks by Paul Chung

Conceptual Bang Nerdlucks by Paul Chung

Conceptual Nerdluck by Uli Meyer

Conceptual Blanko Nerdlucks by Paul Chung

Conceptual Nerdlucks by Dan Root

The Nerdlucks head for
Earth in their spaceship.

Conceptual spaceship by Dan McHugh

Conceptual spaceship by Keith Sparrow

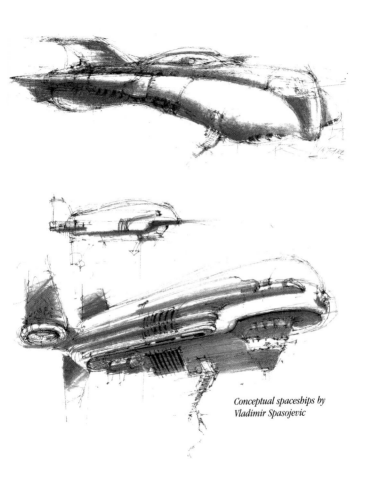

*Conceptual spaceships by
Vladimir Spasojevic*

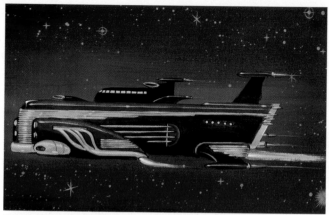

Conceptual spaceship by Bill Wray

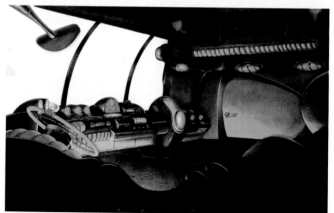

Spaceship interior background painting by James Finn (layout by Gary Mouri)

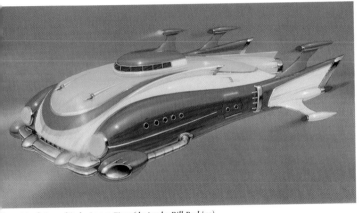

Conceptual spaceship by James Finn (design by Bill Perkins)

Meanwhile on Earth, Michael Jordan — the *crème de les basketball players* — has announced his retirement. He will explore new challenges in golf and baseball.

He's quite good at golf.

His baseball career is, at best, under-whelming, but he's the *only* minor league player with his own publicist, an irritating but good-hearted toady named Stan.

The Nerdlucks crash land in Looney Tune Land. What they lack in stature, they make up for in crummy attitude. The bow-tied, buglike aliens have ray guns and a mission: to take Bugs Bunny and the Looney Tunes hostage. After they've finished laughing, Yosemite Sam balks, and gets zapped. Bugs thinks fast, and demands a chance for his cohorts to defend themselves.

Looney Tune forest layout by Dan Fausett

Looney Tune forest background painting by Raymond Zibach

Overleaf: Conceptual Looney Tune forest by Maurice Hunt

Nawt Nerdluck, Bupkus Nerdluck, and Pound Nerdluck rough animation by Tom Riggin

Blanko Nerdluck rough animation by Holger Leihe

Blanko Nerdluck rough animation by Tom Riggin

*Overleaf: Devastated Looney
Tune forest background
painting by Raymond Zibach
(layout by Dan Fausett)*

Looney Tune Town Hall background painting by James Finn (layout by Lisa Souza)

Looney Tune Town Hall interior layout by Dan Fausett

Overleaf: *Looney Tune Town Hall interior color key by Scott Wills*

The confused Nerdlucks agree. Bugs challenges the stubby aliens to a basketball game. How could the Looney Tunes *lose?* Don't leave yet.

The Nerdlucks may be naive, but they're not stupid. Well, not totally stupid. After studying basketball, they realize (like their boss) that the shortest distance between two points is to steal something.

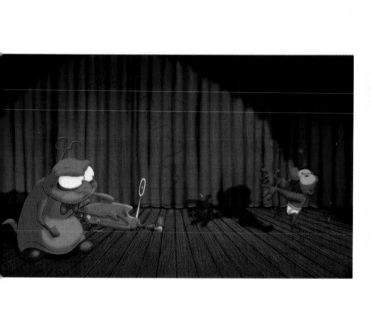

*Bupkus Nerdluck rough animation
by Holger Leibe*

So the Nerdlucks visit stadiums across the country using their superior technology to swipe the talents of five of America's top basketball stars. They leave the world's top players tripping over themselves like fifth-graders at their first square dance.

When they approach the Looney Tunes on the court, the Nerdlucks, with the professional basketball players' talents, are transformed into one part superstar, two parts monster: *Monstars*. They can run, shoot, pass, and drive, all with the arrogance of neighborhood bullies.

Conceptual Nawt Monstar by Tim Watts

Conceptual Bupkus Monstar by Tim Watts and Paul Chung

Conceptual Blanko Monstar by Tim Watts

Conceptual Bank Monstar and head by Bruce Smith

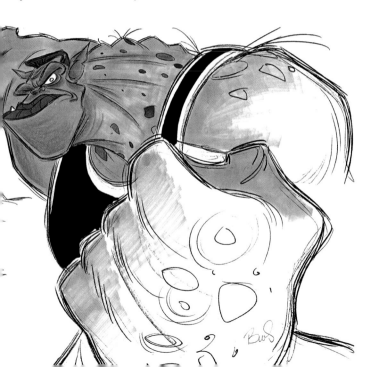

Conceptual Bang Monstar by Tim Watts

Storyboard of Swackhammer and Monstars by Uli Meyer

*Conceptual Bang Monstar
by Tony Cervone*

Already the Looney Tunes are getting a sense of what it's going to be like as slaves on Moron Mountain. They face five Monstars and a lot of bad attitude. Bugs needs help. But where's he going to find it?

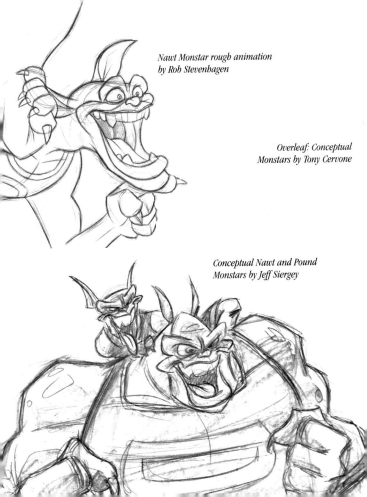

*Nawt Monstar rough animation
by Rob Stevenhagen*

*Overleaf: Conceptual
Monstars by Tony Cervone*

*Conceptual Nawt and Pound
Monstars by Jeff Siergey*

Conceptual basketball court by Bill Wray

Conceptual basketball court by Alex Mann

Conceptual basketball court by Alex Mann

Conceptual basketball court by Gary Mouri

Enter Michael Jordan, the basketball, er, baseball star, er, player. Bugs yanks Michael Jordan off the golf course and hauls him to Looney Tune Land, an animated fantasy world of rabbits, pigs, ducks, and little birds, some of which are now fluttering around Michael's head. Bugs Bunny figures that maybe in person he'll take pity and help them.

Conceptual Michael Jordan
by Dino Athanassiou

Storyboard of Blanko Monstar by Kurt Anderson

Storyboard of Bupkus and Bang Monstars by Kurt Anderson

No dice. "I'm a baseball player now," Michael explains. "Right," Bugs tells him. "And *I'm* a Shakespearean actor."

Michael resists, even after the Monstars have wadded him up and shot a basket with him. But when they get rough with Tweety, it's the last straw for Michael Jordan. "Let's play some basketball," he tells them with his most steely game face.

Bugs Bunny rough animation by Gary Dunn

*Daffy Duck rough animation by
Ken Morrissey*

*Daffy Duck by De
Roberts (rough animatio
and Edmund Perrym
(assistant animatio*

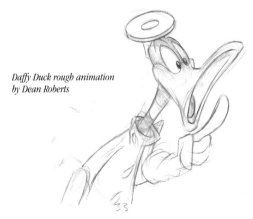

*Daffy Duck rough animation
by Dean Roberts*

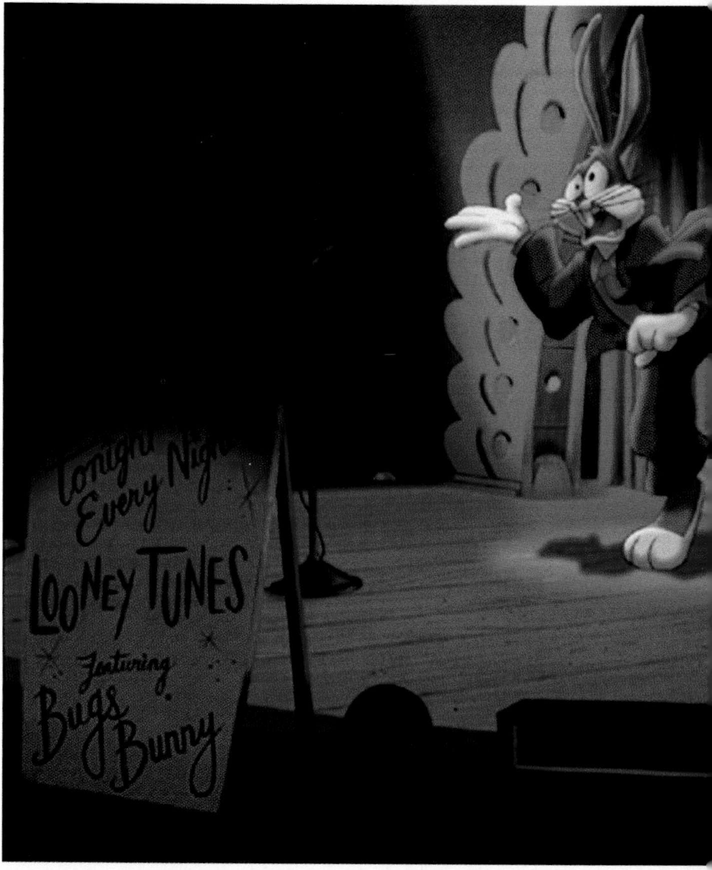
Tonight Every Night
LOONEY TUNES
featuring
Bugs Bunny

Bugs Bunny rough animation by Darren Vandenburg

*Bugs Bunny by Darren
Vandenburg (rough animation)
and Jean Paul Vermuelen
(assistant animation)*

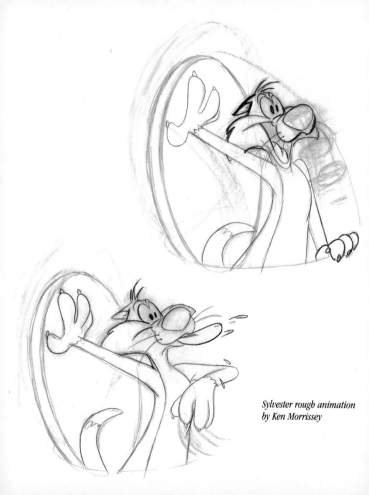

*Sylvester rough animation
by Ken Morrissey*

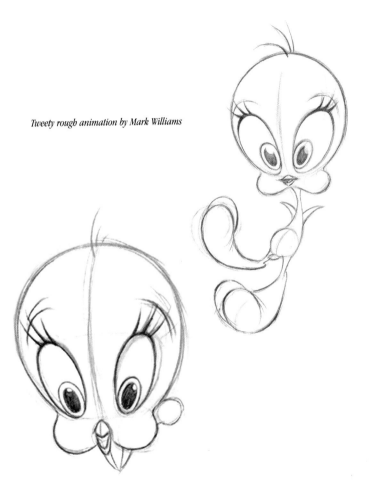

Tweety rough animation by Mark Williams

Part 2

THE JAMS

Sending Bugs and Daffy back to his home in the real world to retrieve his lucky North Carolina basketball shorts, Michael plans his game strategy. After all, the "Tune Squad" has everything: spirit, energy, and enthusiasm. All they lack is talent.

Thermal panel of Michael Jordan and the Looney Tunes by Tony Cervone

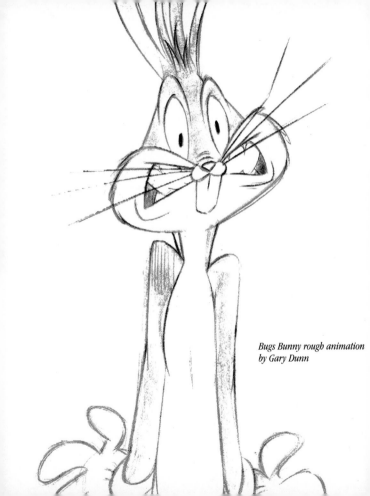

*Bugs Bunny rough animation
by Gary Dunn*

*Daffy Duck rough animation
by Murray Debus*

Sylvester rough animation by Mark Bröcking

Tasmanian Devil rough animation by Andreas Von Adrian

Michael wonders what he's gotten himself into until a young female bunny named Lola wanders onto the court and volunteers to play. After the initial Looney Tune laughter dies down, she stuns everyone with her amazing basketball talents and dazzles Bugs with her amazing good looks.

Conceptual Lola Bunny
by Tony Cervone

Conceptual Lola Bunny by Tony Cervone,
Jeff Siergey, and Ashanti Miller

Dirty practice gym color key by Raymond Zibach (layout by DanMcHugh)

Practice Gym color key by Scott Wills (layout by Gary Mouci)

Lola Bunny thumbnail sketch by Ashanti Miller

*Lola Bunny thumbnail sketches
by Ashanti Miller*

Lola Bunny thumbnail sketch by Ashanti Miller

Lola Bunny thumbnail sketch by Ashanti Miller

The real world of professional basketball is in a state of panic: five great players have lost their talents. Could it be a virus? Bacteria? Other players refuse to enter the stadiums. The commissioner cancels the season.

The victimized stars visit doctors, psychiatrists, even a soothsayer. No one can help them. They're just regular guys now. *Clumsy* regular guys.

After being humiliated on the court by a bunch of little girls, one basketball superstar even returns to church, vowing to change his ways. As he speaks, the Monstars are using his and the others' stolen talents to make pulp out of the Tune Squad in the Ultimate Game.

Part 3

THE
ULTIMATE
GAME

In Looney Tune Land, it's the Tune Squad versus the Monstars, the Ultimate Game in the ultimate stadium to decide who stays and who goes. Did we say "game"? Call it a *rout,* with the Monstars using every devious device at hand to humiliate the Tune Squad.

Conceptual stadium by Neil Ross

Conceptual stadium by Mark Swan

conceptual stadium interior by Raymond Zibach

Conceptual Pound Monstar by Jeff Siergey

The Monstars take bad sportsmanship to a new level, all to the cheers of Swackhammer, who watches from his own private box. Thank goodness for the half-time buzzer, or there wouldn't be a Tune Squad left.

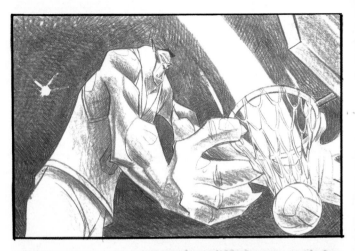

Storyboards of Monstars by Uli Meyer

Conceptual Bang Monstar by Jeff Siergey

Conceptual Nawt Monstar by Jeff Siergey

Conceptual Bang Monstar by Tim Watts

Yosemite Sam and Elmer Fudd rough animation by Jeff Siergey

*Swackhammer rough
animation by
Vladimir Todorov*

Nawt Monstar rough animation by Bruce Smith

Lola Bunny and Bugs Bunny rough animation by Roberto Casale

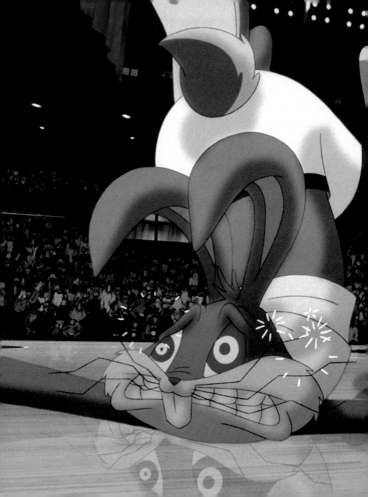

After learning the secret of the Monstars' power (courtesy of poor, battered Stan), Michael calls a meeting in the locker room at halftime. It doesn't help. The Tune Squad is out of tune.

Michael's pep talk about giving your all in the face of defeat just puts his players to sleep. What they need is something special.

Conceptual locker room by Don Reich

...oney Tune locker room background painting by Raymond Zibach (layout by Craig Voigt)

Bugs cleverly labels an ordinary water bottle "Michael's Secret Stuff," and they all drink from it. It gives them what they need to go back into the game: courage. This is the last chance to save themselves from Moron Mountain and the last chance for Michael to get his fellow players' talents back.

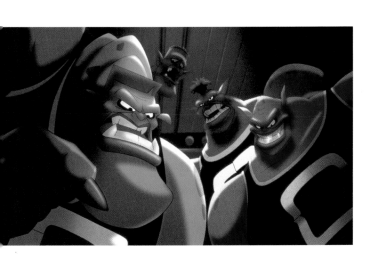

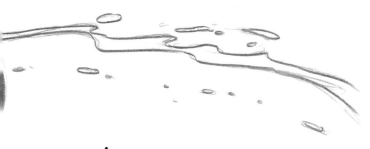

The second half of the game is different. The Tune Squad is a scoring machine, bringing their score up to within one point of the Monstars — but the effort has taken its toll. Michael's team is in tatters, pounded and smashed by their opponents.

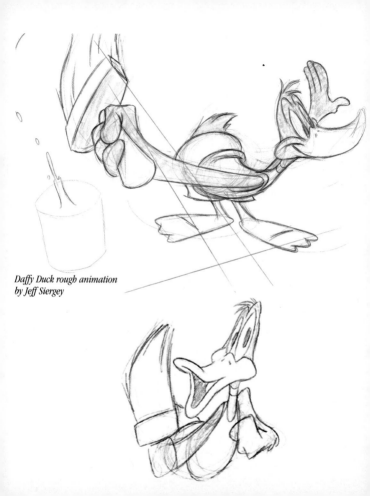

*Daffy Duck rough animation
by Jeff Siergey*

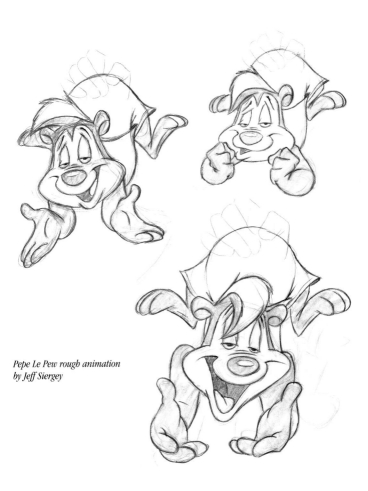

*Pepe Le Pew rough animation
by Jeff Siergey*

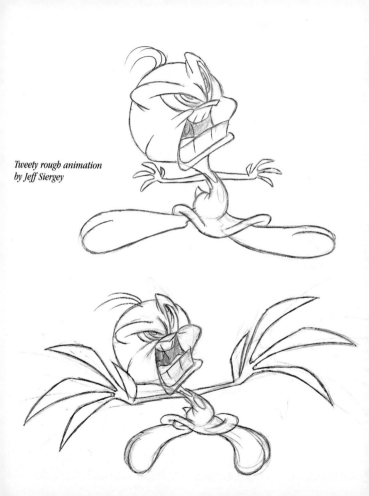

*Tweety rough animation
by Jeff Siergey*

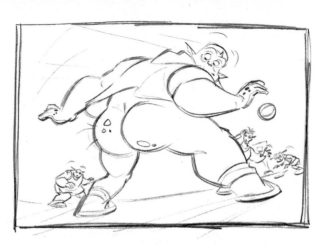

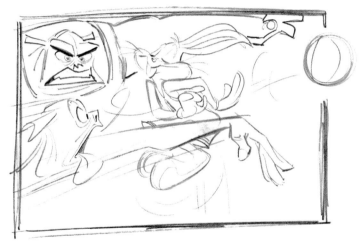

Storyboard of Bugs Bunny and Monstars by Bruce Smith

Lola Bunny rough animation by Gary Dunn

Lola Bunny rough animation by Gary Dunn

Lola Bunny rough animation by Paul Chung

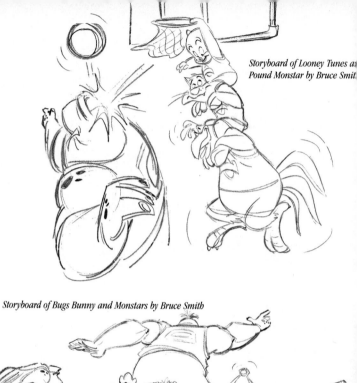

Storyboard of Looney Tunes and Pound Monstar by Bruce Smith

Storyboard of Bugs Bunny and Monstars by Bruce Smith

Swackhammer, sitting in his elaborate visitor's box, goes apoplectic. "I want *him* for Moron Mountain," he shouts, pointing at Michael Jordan.

"If you win, you get me," Michael agrees. Swackhammer laughs like a tickled shark. "You'll sign autographs all day long and play one-on-one with the paying customers. And you'll always lose. Do we have a deal?" "Deal," Michael tells him. Time in.

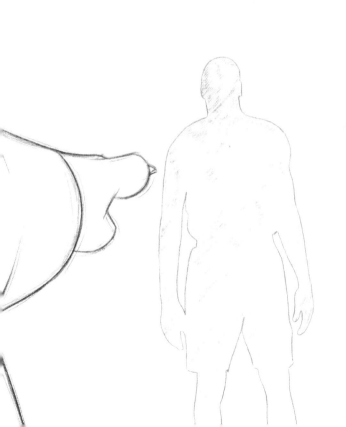

Jackhammer rough animation by Rob Stevenhagen and Simon Ward Horner

Bugs Bunny rough animation by Vincent Woodcock

Ten seconds on the clock. Trailing by a single point. Michael is suddenly aware of the power of the cartoon world, where the physical laws of the real world don't count.

What is flattened pops back. What is blasted comes together again. What can hang in the air can hang in the air longer — can even *bend* the air. Five seconds, four seconds, three. . . . He stretches to the hoop while the Monstars try to hold him down. One second . . . and SLAM! He scores! The Tune Squad wins!

Swackhammer is not happy. "Get in the Spaceship," he bellows. But the Monstars — who now can see clearly that he's been bullying them, realize that they are now bigger than he ever was. They strap him to a rocket and shoot him into outer space. The Looney Tunes are free from the threat of Moron Mountain. The Monstars return the talents to the basketball players again, and stay, as Nerdlucks, in Looney Tune Land.

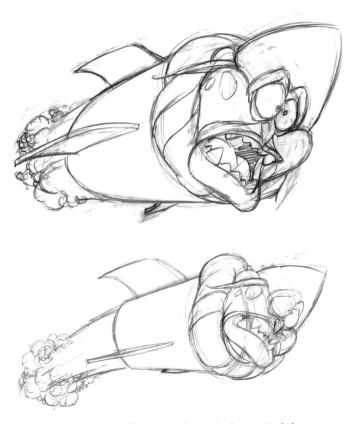

Swackhammer rough animation by Bruce Woodside

And Michael Jordan, his own talents recharged from the whole Space Jam, returns to basketball.

And that's all, folks.

Daffy Duck rough animation by Tom MacGrath